MAKING A BOOK

Mandy Suhr

Thomson Learning
New York

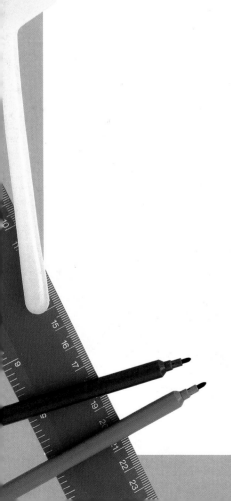

Acknowledgments
The publishers would like to thank the pupils and staff of Leith Walk Primary School in Edinburgh, Scotland, for their help in the production of this book. We also wish to credit the following photographers for taking the photographs used in this book: APM Photographic 16, 17, 18, 24, 25, 28 (top), 33, 34, 35, 36, 37, 38, 39; Angus Blackburn contents page, 4, 5, 8-9, 10, 11, 12, 13, 15, 20, 26; Zul Mukhida cover, 6-7, 19, 21, 22, 27, 29, 30, 31, 32, 40, 41, 42, 43. The illustration on page 28 (bottom) was supplied by John Yates.

Cover: Stacey and Miles make a book.
Contents page: Papinder, Richard, Lindsay, Sarah, and Sasha look through some books to find ideas.

Editor: Deb Elliott
Photo stylist: Zoe Hargreaves
Cover design: Loraine Hayes
Inside design: Malcolm Walker
Production controller: Kate MacKillop

First published in the United States by
Thomson Learning
115 Fifth Avenue
New York, NY 10003

First published in 1993 by
Wayland Publishers Limited

Library of Congress Cataloging-in-Publication Data
Suhr, Mandy.
  Making a book / Mandy Suhr.
        p.   cm.
  Includes bibliographical references and index.
  ISBN 1-56847-103-3 : $15.95
  1. Publishers and publishing—Juvenile literature.
  2. Printing, Practical—Juvenile literature. [1. Books.
  2. Publishers and publishing. 3. Printing.] I. Title.
  Z278.S93   1994   93-38569

Printed in Italy

Contents

An idea

Have you ever read a book that made you laugh out loud? Or a book that let you imagine you were in a distant place? Or one that taught you something useful? If you have, then you know that a good book is magical.

There are two kinds of books: fiction and nonfiction. Fiction books are made up. A book with talking animals and flying teacups is fiction. Nonfiction books are true. A book about how Bill Clinton became president of the United States or how to build a dollhouse is nonfiction.

Fiction and nonfiction books start with the same thing: an idea.

Jordan loves reading books about his favorite subject, art.

The books that you borrow from libraries or buy in stores have been produced by publishing companies. These are businesses that make money by making and selling books.

Publishing companies are always on the lookout for new and exciting ideas for books. Many people who have a good idea send it to a publishing company. The publisher decides which ideas should be developed into books that will be published.

Publishers are sent many ideas each day from hopeful writers. But only a few ideas end up as books.

Many people send more than an idea for a book. They send an entire manuscript to a publishing company. Publishers get thousands of manuscripts every year.

Asma borrows books from her local library every week.

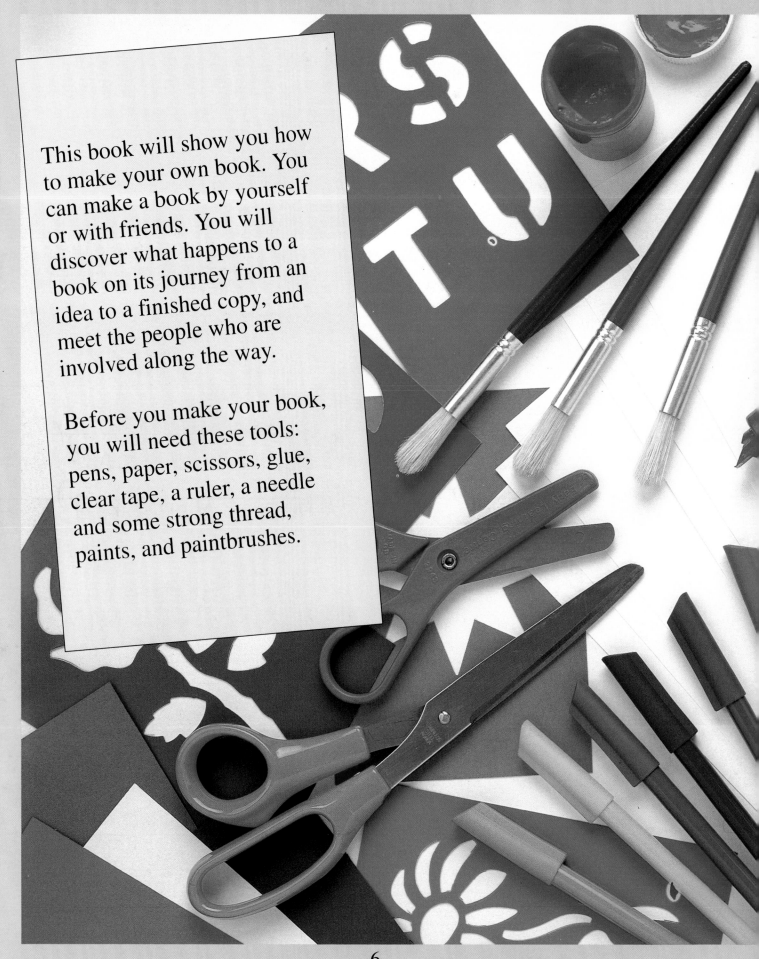

This book will show you how to make your own book. You can make a book by yourself or with friends. You will discover what happens to a book on its journey from an idea to a finished copy, and meet the people who are involved along the way.

Before you make your book, you will need these tools: pens, paper, scissors, glue, clear tape, a ruler, a needle and some strong thread, paints, and paintbrushes.

Researching your idea

You may have a great idea for a book but you are not sure what to do next. Doing some careful thinking will point you in the right direction.

First decide whether your book will be fiction—a made-up story—or nonfiction—a true book that gives information.

Think about fictional stories first. There are lots of different kinds—adventure, humor, and horror, to name a few. Really good stories all have something in common whatever they are about. They have a beginning that sets the scene and tells the reader a little about the characters; a middle where most of the action happens; and an end, which can sometimes be surprising.

If you are going to write fiction, keep these steps in mind. Think

about what you liked in other stories you have read, such as a funny character or spooky setting. You can use these ideas in your story in a different way.

Nonfiction books that give information are a little different. They don't usually have story lines, but they do have some special parts.

Look through lots of books. Which are most interesting and which have the best designs? You can use some of the good ideas from these books in your book.

The index and contents pages are very important in a nonfiction book, because they help the reader find information quickly and easily.

These pages are useful because people don't usually read information books in one sitting. Instead they look for bits of information at different times. Some books also have information boxes, charts, maps, or graphs for quick reference.

At the beginning of a nonfiction book you will usually find a contents page. This lists the heading of each chapter. This helps the reader find a particular piece of information. If the contents page doesn't help, the reader can turn to the index in the back of the book. This lists all the information that is in the book in alphabetical order.

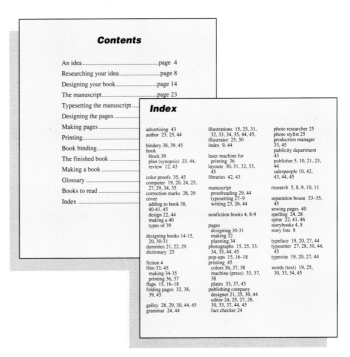

Once you have decided whether to write a fiction or nonfiction book and you have chosen a subject, you must ask yourself: will anybody else want to read it?

This is a very important point for publishing companies to think about, too. They must sell lots of books to make money and stay in business.

If a publishing company likes an idea for a book, it might try to find out how many people will buy a copy. This is called market research. Market research means asking people questions and getting their opinions on what makes a good book. By doing market research, the company can also discover more ideas for books.

Finding out what people want

Asking questions is one of the ways you can find out what types of books people want to read, and what they think of your idea for a book. You can do this at school or with a group of friends.

A questionnaire is a list of questions like these:

1. Do you prefer storybooks or information books?
2. Which subjects do you most like to read about?
3. Which do you prefer: books with more words than pictures or books with more pictures than words?

You can make a questionnaire. If you think carefully about which questions to ask, the answers will give you information you need for research on your own book. Ask people in your group to answer each question while you or a friend takes notes.

Thanks to your questionnaire, you should have more information about what to put in your book.

If you have decided to make a nonfiction book, look at other books on the same subject. You can take notes from these to find information for your own book. Think of a new way to present the information. You can also tell what you think the information means.

When you begin to collect information, remember who you hope will be reading your book. Think about whether they will understand and be interested in the facts you choose.

Think of different ways to present the information in your book.

Write a book review

Choose a book that you have read recently and write a review. List all the good and bad points of the book.

Designing your book

The design of your book is the way it is planned and laid out. This doesn't just mean organizing the words that will go into the book, it means the way the book will look.

The first stage in designing your book is to plan how you will present the information you have collected.

Will your book have photographs? Will it have illustrations? Your book can have both, or it can have no art—only text.

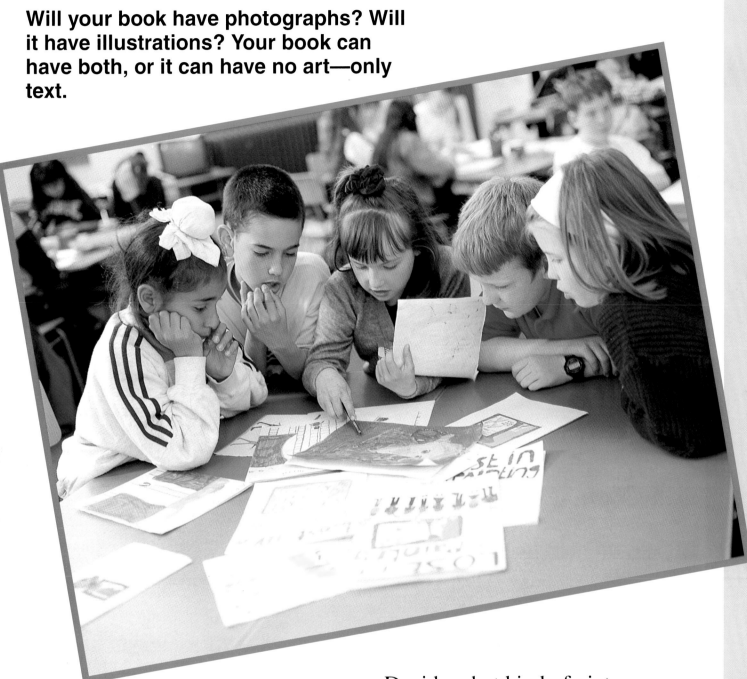

Decide on the size, shape, and number of pages that will be in your book. The instructions in this book are for a twelve-page book, but you may wish to make your book longer.

Decide what kind of pictures you will use. Will your book have illustrations or photographs? Will it have colored borders around the pages? Will it have flaps or pop-ups? Think of ways to make your book eye-catching and different.

Pop-ups and flaps

Pop-ups and flaps can add fun to the pages of your book. This example of a ladybug under a leaf will show you how to make a pop-up and flaps. You can make just about anything jump off a page using this method.

1. Draw a ladybug and two leaves on a piece of brightly colored cardboard. Make one of the leaves big enough to cover the ladybug. The ladybug will be the pop-up and the leaves will be flaps.

2. Cut out the shapes. Be careful when using the scissors.

3. Now make a spring for the ladybug pop-up. Cut a long thin piece of cardboard. Fold the cardboard in half.

4. Fold the cardboard into an accordion shape. To do this, make a half-inch fold at the end of the cardboard. Flip the cardboard over. Fold the same end half an inch again. You should have a spring like the one below.

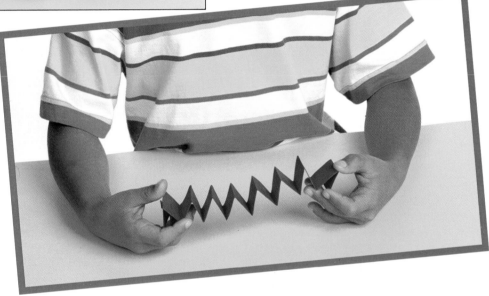

5. Squash down the spring and glue one end to the back of the ladybug.

6. Glue the other end of the spring to the page.

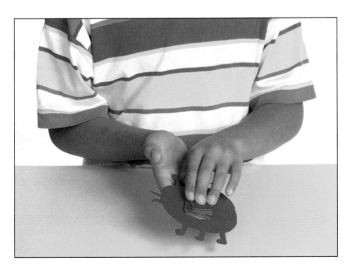

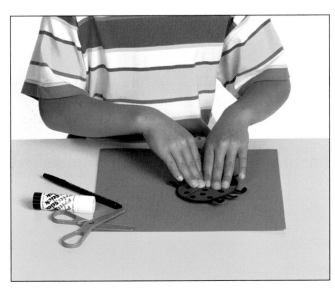

7. Tape the edge of one of the leaves to the cardboard. Make sure the leaf covers the ladybug. This is the flap.

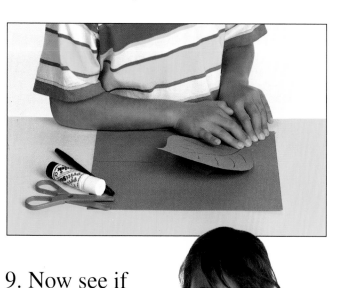

8. Tape down the second leaf. This time the leaf should cover only half the ladybug. This leaf acts as the catch to down hold the flap.

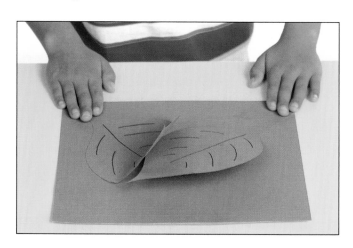

9. Now see if your pop-up and flaps work.

10. Lift the flaps and out pops the ladybug.

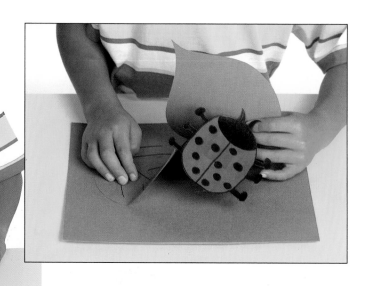

You could use this method to make ghosts pop out of cupboards or monsters jump through windows. You could even make people jump out of bed.

The words

Now it is time to think about the words, or text. Typed or printed text is easier to read than even the neatest handwriting, so try to borrow a typewriter or computer from school or from a friend. Some typewriters and computers can print out different styles of type, or typefaces, which can change the look of your book. You could use a spooky looking typeface to print a scary story.

Computers can also print out different sizes of type. The size of type is more important to the book than you might think. If it is too small, the words will be hard to read. Imagine having to read a whole book with type that size!

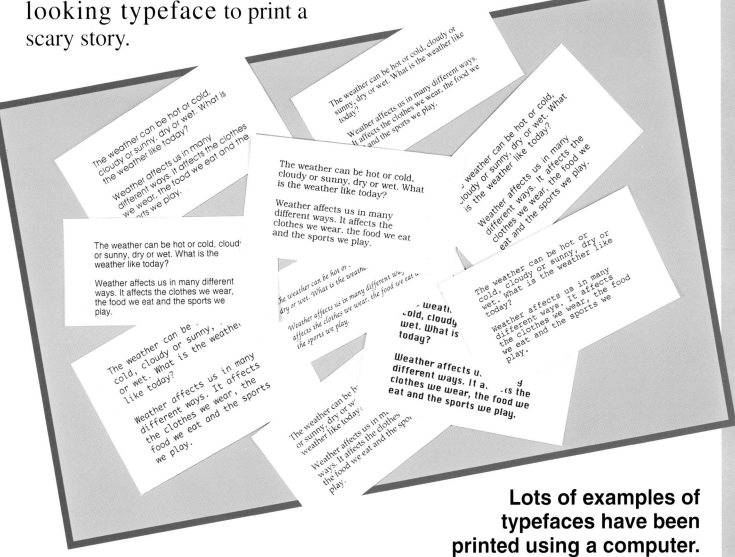

Lots of examples of typefaces have been printed using a computer.

If the type is too big it might seem as if the book is for very young children.

Try different typefaces and sizes on a computer. Pick the one that's right for your book.

Don't forget the pages at the front and back of your book. These pages are called the front matter and endmatter. They also have to be designed and you need to know what to put on them.

This example is called a dummy. It is used to show how the finished book will look.

The publisher has to think of lots of things when choosing which design would be best for a particular book. She or he has to make sure that the readers will like the look of the book and will be able to read it easily.

The person at the publishing company who designs the way a book will look is called the designer. She or he will make several different "roughs" showing how the book might look, and then will show them to the publisher or editor (above).

A rough is a sketch that the designer uses to show how the pictures and text might be arranged. To save time, roughs can be much smaller than the actual book.

After much discussion, one of the roughs will be chosen and the designer will use this to create an example of two sample pages and a cover.

This is the cover design that was chosen for this book. Did you recognize it?

The designer also designs the cover of the book.

Look at covers of different books. What makes you want to pick up a book? Do the pictures and information on a cover help you to choose a book? Don't forget about the back cover and the spine. When a book is on a shelf, the spine is all that can be seen.

Think about all these things when you start to design your cover.

Design a dummy
Try to come up with lots of different designs for the cover and inside of your book.

Show your designs to some friends and ask which they like best.

Design a dummy spread and cover to show how your finished book will look.

The manuscript

The author of a book is the person who writes it. The job of the author is to produce a typewritten, double-spaced manuscript that can be made into a book.

Sometimes after the author gets an idea for a book, the author writes a book plan or synopsis. This is a way of telling in a few words what is going to be in the book. It helps to ensure that nothing important will be left out.

The synopsis is usually sent to the publisher. If the publisher likes it, the publisher offers to pay the author for the whole manuscript. The publisher will make a contract with the author. This states how much the author will be paid and when the finished manuscript is due to the publisher.

Once the contract has been signed, the author starts work. The author may write several versions, or drafts, before feeling happy with the manuscript.

Before you write your manuscript, make a synopsis so you know what will be in your finished book. As you write the final version, think carefully about the words that you are using. Ask yourself these questions:

● Are the words too hard or too easy for the reader?

● Are they put together in an interesting way?

● Are the sentences easy to read, or are they long and rambling?

● Is all the information correct?

The answers to all of these questions are important when you are trying to make your manuscript interesting to your readers.

Sometimes an author may write the final version very quickly, but some manuscripts take many years of writing and rewriting before they are finished.

The final copy of the manuscript is sent to the editor. The editor checks it, making suggestions for improvement, such as cutting parts or rearranging the order in which they are written. The editor makes sure that the writing flows well. Then a copy editor checks the manuscript for spelling mistakes and mistakes in the grammar and punctuation.

If the author has put the manuscript on a computer, she or he can send it to the editor on a disk. The editor can then check the text and make changes using a computer, too.

You could use a friend as your editor. Ask your friend to read your work and suggest ways in which it could be improved.

Above A copy editor checks the text. If the text has a lot of facts, the editor may send it to a fact checker, whose job is to double-check the information.

Opposite The photo stylist for this book is styling a photograph for a book about magic.

The editor and the designer will meet to decide ways in which the text could be illustrated. They must plan which pictures will go with which parts of the text. Some of the pictures may be photographs, but the editor may have to choose an illustrator to draw pictures to go with the words.

Many publishing companies have art departments with photo researchers. Photo researchers will find all the photographs for the book. The photo researcher will send a picture list to special photographic libraries. The libraries send several photographs to the researcher, who chooses a selection. The editor will then choose the pictures for the book from this selection.

Some photographs have to be carefully set up. This is organized by a photo stylist. The photo stylist must find models and props, the items needed for the photograph. Then the photo stylist must find a photographer to take the pictures. At many publishing companies, the designer acts as the photo stylist.

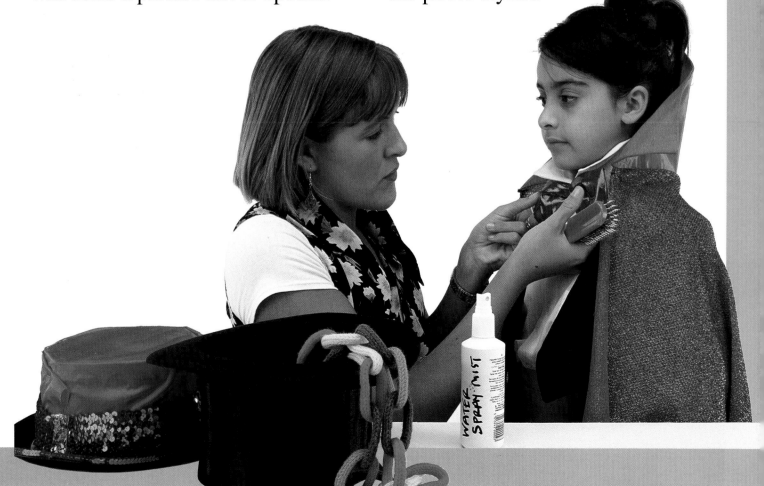

Writing the book

Time to get down to some writing! Collect the tools you will need for the job: a ruler, a pencil, an eraser, and lots of scrap paper. You'll need a dictionary to check the spelling. Write a rough draft first. Then add the fine details and finishing touches. When you are happy with what you have written, type your manuscript onto a computer.

Typesetting the manuscript

Now the editor has helped put the finishing touches on the manuscrfipt. The copy editor has made sure the grammar, punctuation, and spelling are correct. The designer has chosen the typeface and size in which the manuscript will be printed, and the way each page will look.

The next stage is to typeset the manuscript. The person who does this is called the typesetter.

Weather

The weather can be hot or cold, cloudy or sunny, dry or wet. What is the weather like today?

Weather affects us in many different ways. It affects the clothes we wear, the food we eat and the sports we play.

Sunny days make us feel happy, cheerful and warm. The sky is blue and there are few clouds. We wear less clothes so that we stay cool.

Clouds are made from millions of tiny drops of water. The many different shapes of clouds can tell us a lot about the weather.

If the manuscript was typed on a computer, the designer can give the typesetter a disk containing the manuscript. The designer will have marked the text using special marks that tell the typesetter how to type it out. The typesetter has a special computer into which he or she types the words or feeds the disk.

This is the typeface and type size chosen for one book. Do you think they were good choices?

Using the computer, the typesetter can change the type into the size, style, and arrangement that the designer has asked for.

The set type is printed out in long columns of text, called a galley. This is the first version.

It must be checked again by the editor and copy editor for spelling mistakes or other mistakes that might have been made when the manuscript was retyped in the new typeface. Looking for mistakes is called proofreading. The mistakes are called typos.

The copy editor makes corrections for the typesetter. These are called editorial correction marks. There are some examples in the illustration on the right.

CORRECTION MARKS		
MARK IN THE MARGIN	MARK IN THE TEXT	INSTRUCTION
ℰ	ℰ through letter / ℛ through word	remove letter, word
ℰ	ℰ through letter / ℰ through word	remove letter, word and close up the space
a word or letter	∧	add a new letter or word
new letter or new word	∧ through letter / ⋈ through word	change a letter, word, or part of a word
⊙	∧	add a period or a decimal point
⤒(or) ⌃ (or) ⌄	∧	add a comma, semicolon, or colon
C/Ɔ	∧	add parentheses
ⱽⱽ and ⱽⱽ	∧	add quotation marks
=	∧	add a hyphen
u.c.	≡ (under letter)	change the letter to a capital letter
lc	/ through letter	change a capital letter to lower case
⌣	⌣	close up the space between letters or words
#	#	add a space between words
tra.	⌐⌐	change the order of letters or words
rebreak	⌐	move the letter, word, or sentence to the next line, paragraph, or page
t.b.	⌐	take back the letter, word, or sentence to the line, paragraph, or page before
ital.	—— (line) under letter or word	make the letter or word *italic*
b.f.	∿ (squiggly line) under letter/word	make the letter or word **bold**

Opposite **A typesetter uses a computer to make changes to the disk.**

Proofreading your manuscript

Now it's your turn to be an editor. Print out your manuscript making sure that it is the correct line width to fit on the page. This is where your dummy will be useful as a guide for size. You can use a computer or a typewriter. Don't forget to proofread it afterward for typos. Mark any corrections on your galleys with the correct editorial correction marks.

Designing the pages

Once the editor and copy editor have checked the galley, a set is given to the designer.

It is the designer's job to make rough pages, called layouts, to show how the words and pictures will fit together.

The designer cuts up the galley text and arranges it on the rough pages. This can also be done on a computer with a special design program.

The designer marks where the pictures will go and how big they will be. Then the layouts are passed back to the editor.

The layouts are very useful. They show the editor how the pages of the finished book will look. By using the layouts, the designer can tell the illustrator exactly what size the pictures need to be so they will fit. They will show the typesetter how to arrange the final text, too.

Making rough pages
Use your printed text as a galley to make page layouts. If you have typed the text you should photocopy it before you cut it up.

Cut up your galleys and arrange the words and pictures on rough pages. Make sure you use the same number of pages that you have planned for your finished book, using the first page as the title page. Make sure to put the right text next to the right picture. Read it carefully before taping it down.
Mark the place where each

pictures and tape those down instead.

Draw any illustrations that you will put in the final book, using the page layouts to check for size and fit.

Finally, using your page layouts as a guide, make any changes to the arrangement of the text before you print out the finished version. Leave spaces in the text where it will be cut to go on each page.

picture will go but don't tape the pictures down: you will need them for the real book.
You can make photocopies of the

Making pages

Final pages

Now it is time to make your final pages. Choose the paper you wish to use and cut out the correct number of double pages, called spreads. For a 12-page book you will need six pieces of paper made into three spreads.

Put the pages together and fold them. Number them neatly once they are folded together so they won't get mixed up. Use your page layouts to help you tape down the text and pictures in the right places.

The production manager checks the page layouts, photographs, and illustrations before sending them to a reproduction house.

Because you are producing only one book it is easy to do all of the work by hand, but most publishers produce thousands of copies of a book at one time. It would be impossible to produce all of these by hand, so they are printed in factories on large printing machines.

At the publishing company it is the production manager who organizes the printing of the books.

The designer passes the final page layouts to the production manager. She or he checks these and then sends them to a color separator. This is where film of the text, photographs, and illustrations is made.

The film will be used by the printer to make printing plates for the large printing machines.

Making film

There are two ways of positioning color to make film at a separation house.

On the right you can see the way color film has been positioned for many years. All the color tints for borders or boxes, the photographs, illustrations, and text are positioned by hand.

The photograph on the left shows another way to separate color to make film.

The color photographs are loaded onto a machine called a scanner. The scanner spins around very fast, and all the color is separated into blue, red, yellow, and black.

This information is then sent to a computer, which positions the text and all the color on pages very quickly and easily.

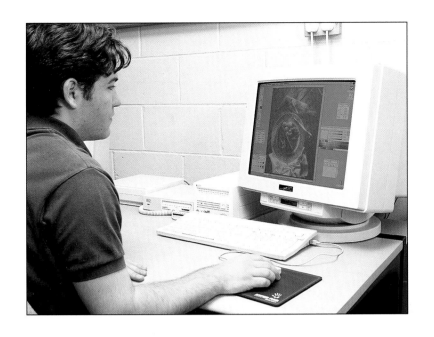

Left The photographs and illustrations can be seen on a computer screen. Any marks or scratches on the film can be corrected.

Once the film is ready, workers make "proofs." These are "proof" that everything has been positioned correctly on the film.

Proofs are sheets of paper with the pictures and text printed on them. Only a few copies are made at the proof stage in case there are still mistakes that need to be corrected.

In the photograph we can see someone checking the film while two other people make proofs. The proofs are sent to the publishing company to be checked by the editor, the designer, and the production manager.

Printing

A book may have many colors on its pages, but it is printed using only four—red, blue, yellow, and black. These colors are mixed together to make all the other colors.

At the reproduction house a special machine is used to make four different films (below), like stencils of the book. Each piece of film is for one of the four printing colors. When these colors are put together, they make all the colors in the book.

Above **The color film is checked before being sent to the printer.**

The films are used to make printing plates at the printer: one to print blue (cyan) ink, one to print red (magenta) ink, one to print yellow ink, and one to print black ink.

The printing machines are so big that they can print many pages at once. The printer arranges the film so that the pages are in the right order, then makes four huge printing plates that will print all the pages at once, one for each color.

Before printing, the printer makes a test proof, called a blueprint, of all the pages. The editor checks that all the information on the pages is in the right place. If all is well, the printing goes ahead.

Huge sheets of paper are fed into one end of the printing machine.

As the paper goes through the printing machine, which is also called the press, it passes over the four printing plates. Each of these plates is covered with colored ink, one for each of the four printing colors.

The paper is printed with each color in turn: first the blue, then red, then yellow, and finally black.

When the printed paper comes out at the other end of the press, it is stacked in piles, called bales, and left to dry (above).

Now the paper is ready to be folded and cut into pages, which are then joined together. The cover will be added last. All this takes place at another factory, called a bindery.

Book binding

At the bindery, the printed sheets are fed into a machine that folds them into pages, and then sorts the pages into the correct order for the book.

The folded pages are fed into another machine, which gathers and trims them to make a book block. The pages in the book block are now in the correct order and are the correct size. The pages of the book block are glued or sewn together.

The final part of the book, the cover, is glued to the book block. The cover must be strong enough to protect the pages. Some books have paper covers, which are softer and cheaper to make. Although hard covers cost more, they are much stronger.

The finished books are taken by truck to a warehouse where they are stored until they are needed.

The pages are sewn together to make the finished book.

Binding your book

Add one more double page of colored paper, the same size as the rest of your pages, to the outside of your book. This will form the end papers, which attach the pages to the cover. Sew your pages down the fold in the middle.

Use some strong thread and a large needle to sew along the fold. Hold the pages together tightly as you do this. Finish by tying the thread securely at the back of the pages, so that the knots will not be seen when the pages are opened.

Make a hard cover from two pieces of strong cardboard. Cut the cardboard about a quarter inch bigger all around than your pages. Cover the cardboard with colored paper.

Use strong, wide tape (about 1½ inches wide) to join or bind the two covers. This will form the spine of the book. Tuck it over at each end to make a neat edge.

Position the pages inside your cover. Stick the colored endpapers down to join the pages to the cover.

Finally, transfer your planned design to your cover. Don't forget to add all the information you would find on a real book cover, such as the title and price. You may want to tape a picture of yourself, the author, to the back cover.

The finished book

If you have finished the project in this book, you will have a book that might be enjoyed by other people. It is special because you have made it yourself. You may want to keep it or give it as a present.

The books made by a publishing company are stored in a huge warehouse. They still have a long way to go before they find a home.

Salespeople will sell the books to stores, libraries, and schools so that many people will be able to read them. The books will travel all over the world once they have been sold.

Advertise your book

Now that you have made your book, you might want other people to know about it. Imagine you want to sell copies of your book. What will you do to advertise it? You can make some posters with information about how wonderful your book is. You can also make leaflets to hand out, or buttons. The list is endless.

Copies of this book have been sold in the United States, Australia, Canada, all over Europe and Africa, and in many other parts of the world. Many different people will make a book when they finish reading this one.

To help to sell the book, the publicity department at the publishing company makes sure lots of people know about it. Copies are sent to newspapers and magazines so that the book can be reviewed.

Sometimes the marketing department makes posters and leaflets to advertise the book. These help the salespeople to sell lots of copies, so that enough money will be made to cover the cost of producing the book.

Now you know a little more about how a book is made. Next time you pick up a book in a store or a library think about the journey it has made and all the people who have helped along the way. Happy reading!

Making a book

Publishing companies are organized differently and have their own systems of book production. This chart shows one way to make a book.

Publisher or author thinks of an idea.

Salespeople carry out some research.

The author writes a book plan. When the publisher agrees with the book plan, the author writes the manuscript.

The designer comes up with roughs to show some different ways the book could look.

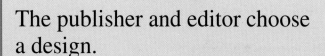

The publisher and editor choose a design.

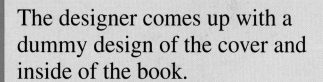

The designer comes up with a dummy design of the cover and inside of the book.

The editor and copy editor check the manuscript for mistakes in spelling and grammar.

The editor and author decide which pictures to use in the book, and the art department starts to find photographs and illustrations.

The designer marks up the manuscript and sends it to the typesetter.

The typesetter produces a galley that shows the manuscript in the right typeface and size.

The designer designs the book using the galleys and any pictures the editor has chosen.

The editor proofreads the galleys and makes any necessary changes called for by the design. The index and captions to the pictures are written, checked, and returned with the galley to the typesetter.

The typesetter makes final corrections and returns a second set of galleys to the editor. When the editor and copy editor have checked these and made no further changes, the typesetter prints the text on pages of film.

▼ ▼

The editor checks that all the pictures are the correct size and then passes them, together with the page layouts, to the production manager.

▼ ▼

The production manager sends the pictures and text film to the separation house.

▼ ▼

At the separation house the text, photographs, and illustrations are put on film. This blue, red, yellow, and black film is joined with the text film to make color proofs. A color proof of the cover is also made.

▼ ▼

The color proofs are checked by the editor, designer, and production manager. Corrections are made, and the corrected film is sent to the printer.

▼ ▼

The color proofs are used by the printer to make plates. The printer makes a blueprint before printing. This is checked by the editor and production manager. If all is correct, the printing goes ahead.

▼ ▼

The printed sheets are sent to the bindery. Here, they are folded, cut, and sewn together. Finally, the cover is added.

▼ ▼

The finished books are stored in a warehouse.

▼ ▼

The salespeople sell copies of the book to stores, schools, and libraries.

Glossary

advertise To let people know about something for sale, using posters, leaflets, or buttons, for example.

bindery The factory where the pages of the book are folded, trimmed to the right size, sewn or glued together, and the covers are added.

book review When people called reviewers write in magazines and newspapers what they thought about a book. Book reviews are important—if a reviewer writes bad things about a book, people might not buy it.

captions The pieces of text that go with illustrations and photographs to explain what they are about.

contract A written agreement between an author or artist and a publishing company. It states how much the author or artist will be paid and when the manuscript or artwork is to be delivered. It is a legal agreement.

film Thin sheets of clear material that have a special coating. They can be photographed easily.

grammar The correct way in which words should be written and spoken.

illustrations The pictures in a book that have been drawn by an artist or illustrator.

punctuation Marks, such as commas and periods, that make writing easier to read and understand.

research Finding out if people are interested in your book, and if not why. Also finding out what books people like.

separation house The factory where all the color—borders, boxes, photographs, and illustrations—are positioned for making film, and where color proofs are made.

spine The part of a book that joins the front and back covers and the inside pages.

stencils The design or pattern made by rubbing ink or paint over the cut-out parts of metal or cardboard.

story line A storybook has a beginning, a middle, and an end. The story line in a book joins these together.

synopsis A book plan that gives a summary of the story or information in a book.

title page The page at the beginning of a book that states the title, author, and publisher. It is often the very first page of a book.

Books to read

Aliki. *How a Book Is Made.* New York: The Trumpet Club, 1986.

Benjamin, Carol L. *Writing for Kids.* New York: HarperCollins Children's Books, 1985.

Merrison, Tim. *Books.* Ada, OK: Garrett Educational Corp., 1991.

Merrison, Tim. *Comics and Magazines.* Ada, OK: Garrett Educational Corp., 1991.

O'Brien-Palmer, Michelle. *Book-Write: A Creative Bookmaking Guide for Young Authors.* Woodinville, WA: MicNik Publications, 1992.

O'Reilly, Susie. *Papermaking.* Arts & Crafts. New York: Thomson Learning, 1994.

Tachell, Judy. *How to Draw Cartoons and Caricatures.* Tulsa: EDC Publishing, 1987.

Index